Building A Successful Business & Brand

I0490884

Introduction

After many years of clocking in and out on a job, I've learned a thing or two about the work field. Because I have felt the pain of being under poor leadership, I thought it wise to write a book about practical tips that could help someone jump start their business. I've heard and experienced firsthand the concerns of the employees because I was one. The Bible says in Proverbs 29:2 which I have seen to be true, "If you show to me a good ruler, I will show you happy people. If you show to me a bad ruler, I will show to you sad people." There is a right way to lead and there is a wrong way to lead. In this book are tried and true principles that have worked for years to solidify many of the prominent businesses we see today. If put into action these principles can help you establish and maintain a successful business too.

Tip #1

Identify your intentions for your company

In other words what is it that you are selling or servicing to contribute to the needs of others.

This sets a foundation for your business/company and it will give you clear direction on how you plan to service your customers and who you plan to serve.

Your product or service is only as good as the need is for it. People want to know what your product or service can do for them, how can it improve their lives.

Sell or service what you are passionate about & you'll always keep an interest in it. Don't just think in terms of earning money, think more in terms of who can this help and the money will automatically come as you help meet the needs of others. So, setting a good foundation, sets the tone for establishing as well as maintaining a successful business. Ask a carpenter, they'll tell you.

Tip #2

Know every position you will need filled and what the duties of that position are

Now that you know what you are selling/servicing, no man is an island, you'll need help. Just as the body is made up with many functional and needful parts to operate at a healthy level, your business is made up of many positions and you're going to need someone to fill those positions. By being able to identify those areas, you are able to hire the people you need for a functional and needful part in the success of your business.

If you are just starting out, chances are you may not be able to hire someone right now and that's okay. You will be filling every position until you are in the position to bring other people on board. By identifying the positions now, it puts you in a position of knowing exactly what you need and exactly at what level you need it. If need be ask around, you'll be surprised at how many people that are willing to help you for little or no expense.

Tip #3

Be cautious of hiring friends & family

Respect is key. What one does another will follow. Separating personal life from business is sometimes difficult to do.

Working with family members could put a strain on your relationship.

Unrealistic expectations of your family member and vice versa as well as discipling difficulties.

Be open but mindful, the dynamics of your relationship changes once you become the Boss and they become the Employee, these dynamics doesn't always work out for the best.

Tip #4

Proper training is key

If you want your employees to perform at an elite level or up to your standards, then proper training should be made available. You can't expect your employees to excel, if you haven't equipped them to succeed. Their performance will reflect your leadership.

Tip #5

Everyone is due the same level of fairness and respect

I know that this sounds elementary, but you'll be surprised at how often this rule of thumb becomes the rotten apple that spoils the bunch.

Respect goes a long way. Favoritism on the other hand will diminish people's respect for you and your company. It threatens your integrity and will reck havoc within your company. Favoritism can influence high turnover rates, poor performance, and you a bad reputation. These things can then threaten the life and legacy of your company. It's the small foxes that often destroys the vine.

Tip #6
Be the example you want to see

Everyone is looking at what you do, you are after all the leader. You want your employees to show up on time, you need to be on time. Whatever you ask, be willing to give. No one will work harder for you then you, be the measuring stick in which they measure their performance by.

Tip #7
Show appreciation
Keep up the morale

Appreciation goes a long way. Whenever we feel appreciated, we have a desire to want to go the extra mile. Yes, it's true you are paying your employees to work for you, but if you have a great team, you should be appreciative. Remember your team could take their skills and talents elsewhere, they are not obligated to work under you. Employee recognition doesn't hurt you or the company in any way, instead, it strengthens it and grows it. We all desire to be apart of something, especially something great. People are least likely to leave something that's great, instead, they are willing to commit long term.

Work is work but it doesn't have to be dull. Incorporating things as such but not limited to: company picnics, bring a child to work day (if you can), favorite team day, trip giveaways, company Christmas parties, company Thanksgiving dinners, small incentives, etc. can help boost the morale in the workplace and cultivate a great work team. However, don't go in the hole to do it, having/following a business budget is paramount to keeping your business afloat. Decide what you can do now, and don't forget to be creative.

Tip #8

Offer health care

If you are just starting out you may not offer health care but if you have at least 50 employees, by law you are required to offer it. As soon as you can, it is in your best interest that you do. You can check small business health insurance options for insurance options for your company.

Not many people will work for a company long term without any benefits. They may be there now but they may not be there for long. Most people won't even consider jobs that doesn't offer health care.

Take care of your employees, they are assets not liabilities.

Tip #9

Offer sick days, not just PTO

Your employees should not have to use PTO days for a sick day off. Would you want to utilize a vacation day as a sick day? It's called vacation days for a reason. Can you imagine planning a trip with your family, then having to cancel because you have utilized most of your days because you were out sick. Sick days, bereavement days, and vacation days can reduce turnovers and call offs.

Tip #10

Hire from within the company first

Each position within the company is a job. If someone leaves or is fired you must replace them. Hiring from within first gives those that are currently working for you a chance to move up or into a different department. This could be the promotion they were wanting. It shows that you encourage growth. That you respect them for wanting to try new things and for being willing to move up within the company. Offer from within first.

Tip #11

Don't be afraid to fire the weak link

It's not the water that's surrounding the boat that sinks it, it's the hole that's in the boat. Every person has a part to play and when that part isn't played it puts a strain on all other parts. Consistent inconsistence in job performance is a red flag. Reprimands are suggested their behavior should be addressed, paper work creates a paper trail, but if issue isn't resolved I suggest you throw Jonah over the boat before Jonah causes the boat to go under.

Tip #12

Challenge your employees to invest in themselves

Invite someone to speak to your team, someone who is influential, a motivator.

Post books through your company email or whatever two way communications outlet you have as suggestions for great books they could possibly read.

If you are a small business and just starting out and are now employing jobs, you may not have a large budget for a well-known speaker and that's okay. Choose someone that is local that is doing things at an elite level that you find useful for your team to glean from.

You're giving back and passing on, encourage them to take on the challenge of investing into themselves.

Tip #13
Don't be afraid of a suggestion box

Your employees are on the floors, in the office, & in the field. They know first hand what they deal with and face on a daily basis. Who better to take suggestions from? A suggestion box posted in a place that the employees have easy access to, checked twice a month would be my suggestion. Please fill free to come up with your own ideas of doing this. However, be open to their suggestions and try not to take it personal or become defensive. Some of their suggestions may not be useful, but some of them just might be the thing that will propel your business. We are all ever learning. Be open to suggestions.

Tip #14
When an employee's suggestion pays off

If an employee suggestion makes your business better, sells increase as a result of you implementing their idea. The morale in the work place increases and reduces turnover rates. Their suggestion saves the company money. It gives you new ideas for improving the product or service. Find ways to reward them. Obviously, they are there to see you win. Let them know how apart of the win they are and how appreciative you are for having them on your team.

Tip #15
Communicate with your employees

Your employees aren't robots, they are people and people thrive off of relationship.

Your employees should not hear more about the company from the news, the community, or third-party affiliate. They should hear it from you. As much as possible keep them informed. Relationship & respect goes a long way.

Tip #16

Trust who you hired

If you hired them, trust them to do the job. No hovering.

Please understand, I'm not saying don't supervise or evaluate performance. I am saying the employee shouldn't be shadowed every minute of every day. You've hired them because you believed they were capable of getting the job done, allow them to do it. Worst case scenario, at the end of their sixty- or ninety-day probation they didn't live up to your expectations and now the job is back available.

Tip #17

Pray

Pray over your business and the employees.

Pray that you'll attract the people you need as your journey continues of exploring and fulfilling your purpose.

Be grateful for being able to aid someone in their time of need.

Be grateful in all things.

Ask for wisdom because you're going to need it.

Trust in the Lord with all your heart and lean not to your own understanding.

Tip #18

Evaluate job performance

Pay attention to your employees strengthens and weaknesses (this will be a job for a supervisor but you may have to do it, just depending upon the size of the staff). One employee might perform poorly on one job and another on another job, but if you switch the two up they might excel. Poor performance in one area could be a strength in another. Find out where your employees fit in best by periodically evaluating them, and you'll almost always receive stellar performance.

Tip #19

Take risks

It is a guarantee that you miss one hundred of the chances you don't take.

Don't be afraid to bring different things to the table.

Don't be afraid to expand your market or to diversify if you feel the need to. Nothing can kill a company faster than "we've always done it this way". Traditions are nice as long as they are working for you and are in line with your core principles. They are not okay when they stifle your growth and keep you from expressing your truth. What worked then, may not work now. Change happens whether we like it or not. Be open to change.

Tip #20

Give back

It is more blessed/enjoyable to give than to receive.

As much as you give it will be given back to you.

Be light into someone's darkness in more ways than one.

Tip #21

Never stop growing

Grow as much as you can. Your business can only go as far as you can take it.

Tip #22

All hands on deck

If you are a small business, don't fail to help where needed, especially if you can't afford to hire extra man power.

Tip #23

Don't make big decisions on your own

Try not to make decisions without gathering necessary information, to do so is folly.

Never be rushed into decision making.

Your emotions are your guiding light, allow it to inform you concerning the decisions you make.

If you have a board, close friend, or family member that have your best interest at heart, consult with them if you feel you must but always follow your strong inclination to make the decision that you feel you must.

Allow God to bring wisdom to your dilemma at any time.

A wise man seeks counsel.

Tip #24

A workman or woman is worthy of his or her wages

Would you want decent wages?

Many people are distracted from their work because they are searching for new work all for better pay.

If a man or woman does the work, they should at least get paid well for it.

Tip #25

Don't seek counsel among thorns

Don't seek counsel among those that you know aren't looking out for your good.

Don't ignore your intuition.

Seeking advice from those that aren't interested in your success is not wise. Their advice is their device for your demise.

Tip #26

Make connections

No man is an island.

Be resourceful.

Be approachable. Put yourself out there.

Become more interested in making friends than enemies.

Don't be afraid to ask for help.

Tip #27

No call no show equals AWOL

Unless there is a medical emergency that can be verified, suspension without pay can be one way to get your point across that that type of behavior is unacceptable. If the employee demonstrates this type of behavior again, termination should be the consequence. Abandonment of their job is disrespectful and unreliable behavior. It is inconsiderate and strenuous upon others that must carry their load in their absence.

Work the principles that are listed in this book and they will surely work for you. Much success!

Write your overall vision for your company or business.

Notes

Write your S.M.A.R.T. goals for the year and even up to five years if you can.

Notes

What are some things you've already accomplished?

_____

_____

_____

Notes

Think of some things/habits that could cause your business to crumble.

_____

_____

_____

_____

_____

_____

_____

_____

_____

_____

_____

_____

_____

_____

_____

_____

_____

_____

_____

_____

_____

_____

_____

_____

_____

_____

_____

_____

_____

_____

_____

_____

_____

_____

_____

_____

_____

Notes

List preventative action steps towards slips and falls from previous question. This could also lead to a company policy and/or a mission statement.

_____

_____

_____

_____

_____

_____

_____

_____

_____

_____

_____

_____

_____

_____

_____

_____

_____

_____

_____

_____

_____

_____

_____

_____

_____

_____

_____

_____

_____

_____

_____

_____

_____

_____

Notes

In what ways can you continue to develop yourself for the good of your business/company?

_____

_____

_____

_____

_____

_____

_____

_____

_____

_____

_____

_____

_____

_____

_____

_____

_____

_____

_____

_____

_____

_____

_____

_____

_____

_____

_____

_____

_____

_____

Notes

What are some resources that you may already have but may not have noticed?

Notes

Books to read

_____

_____

_____

_____

Notes

List your mentors and tell why they are your mentors.

_____

_____

_____

_____

_____

_____

_____

_____

_____

_____

_____

_____

_____

_____

_____

_____

_____

_____

_____

_____

_____

_____

_____

_____

_____

_____

_____

_____

_____

_____

_____
_____
_____
_____

Notes

Write your strong why for your product or service.

_____
_____
_____
_____
_____
_____
_____
_____
_____
_____
_____
_____
_____
_____
_____
_____
_____
_____
_____
_____
_____
_____
_____
_____
_____
_____
_____
_____

Notes

What is the brand/legacy you want for yourself?

Notes